T0394805

BARREL RACING

BY RACHEL GRACK

AMICUS LEARNING

What are you

curious about?

Curious About is published by
Amicus Learning, an imprint of Amicus
P.O. Box 227, Mankato, MN 56002
www.amicuspublishing.us

Editors: Ana Brauer and Megan Siewert
Series Designer: Kathleen Petelinsek
Book Designer and Photo Researcher: Emily Dietz

Library of Congress Cataloging-in-Publication Data
Names: Koestler-Grack, Rachel A., 1973– author.
Title: Curious about barrel racing / by Rachel Grack.
Description: Mankato, MN : Curious About is published by
Amicus Learning, [2025] | Series: Curious about Rodeo |
Includes bibliographical references and index. | Audience:
Ages 6–9 years | Audience: Grades 2–3 | Summary: "Learn how
cowboys and cowgirls (and their horses) compete in barrel racing
rodeo events in this question-and-answer book for elementary-aged
readers. Includes infographics and back matter to support research
skills, along with table of contents, glossary, books and websites
for further research, and index"— Provided by publisher.
Identifiers: LCCN 2024015033 (print) | LCCN
2024015034 (ebook) | ISBN 9798892000840
(lib bdg) | ISBN 9798892001427 (paperback)
| ISBN 9798892002004 (ebook)
Subjects: LCSH: Barrel racing—Juvenile literature.
Classification: LCC GV1834.45.B35 K64 2025
(print) | LCC GV1834.45.B35 (ebook) |
DDC 791.8/4—dc23/eng/20240508
LC record available at https://lccn.loc.gov/2024015033
LC ebook record available at https://lccn.loc.gov/2024015034

Photo Credits: Alamy Stock Photo/Arco / P. Mette, 9, H. Mark
Weidman Photography, 19; Dreamstime/Onepony, 3, 20–21,
Slowmotiongli, 9; Getty Images/Dan Peled, 2, 12, georgeclerk,
4-5, Houston Chronicle/Hearst Newspapers, 6, Maddie Meyer,
2, 8, maiteali, 13, THEPALMER, 7, 10, Xinhua News Agency, 15;
Pexels/@coldbeer, cover, 1; Shutterstock/Brett Holmes, 16–17,
from O, 9, Jana Mackova, 9, zorina_larisa, 14; The Noun
Project/Andy Horvath, 22, 23, Mohamed Mb, 22, 23

Printed in China

CHAPTER THREE

Bringing Home the Win
PAGE
16

What is barrel racing?

It's a type of horse race held at rodeos. A horse gallops down the **alleyway**. It charges through the gate. The race is on! The track runs around three barrels. Riders take turns circling them in a cloverleaf pattern. The fastest time wins.

At rodeos, contestants perform roping and riding skills.

Barrel racing is a women's rodeo sport.

Who can race?

Some rodeos also have a teen class for riders ages 13 to 18.

Only women barrel race in **professional** rodeos. But both girls and boys can race in youth and **amateur** events. Riders are grouped by age. The junior class includes riders ages nine to 12. Kids eight and under race in the peewee class.

Which kind of horse is best at barrel racing?

Many barrel racers choose to ride American Quarter horses.

Any horse can race. But some **breeds** are faster and easier to train. The most popular barrel racers are American Quarter Horses. They are athletic and strong. They can stop quickly, make sharp turns, and take off in a blast. But other horses make winning racers, too.

QUARTER HORSE
FAST, ATHLETIC, GENTLE

1

PAINT HORSE
FRIENDLY, STRONG, FAST

2

THOROUGHBRED
SMART, BOLD, STRONG

3

APPALOOSA
EASY-GOING, LOYAL, BRAVE

4

ARABIAN
FAST, ATHLETIC, HIGH ENERGY

5

BARREL RACING BREEDS

How do riders circle the barrels?

The barrels are set up in a triangle shape. Its base faces the alleyway. The race follows a cloverleaf pattern. The horse runs three tight turns at full speed. Riders can start with either barrel. They must complete the pattern and bolt to the finish line.

BARREL RACE PATTERNS

LEFT BARREL FIRST

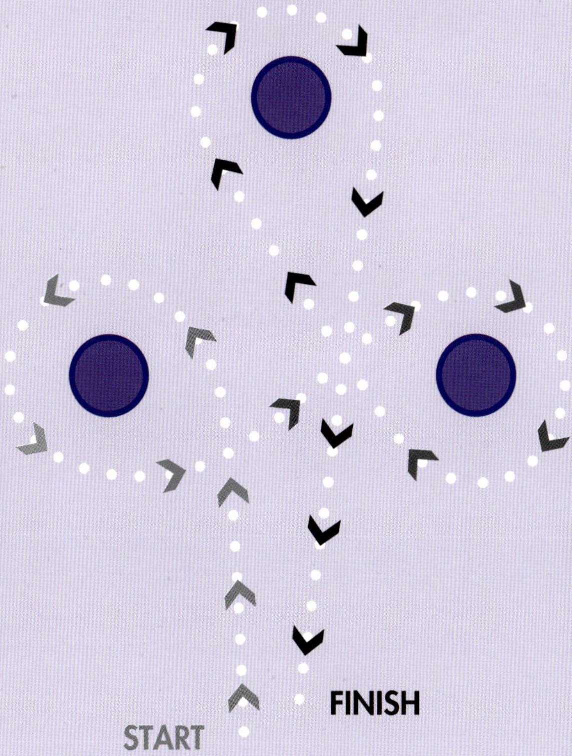

START

FINISH

RIGHT BARREL FIRST

FINISH

START

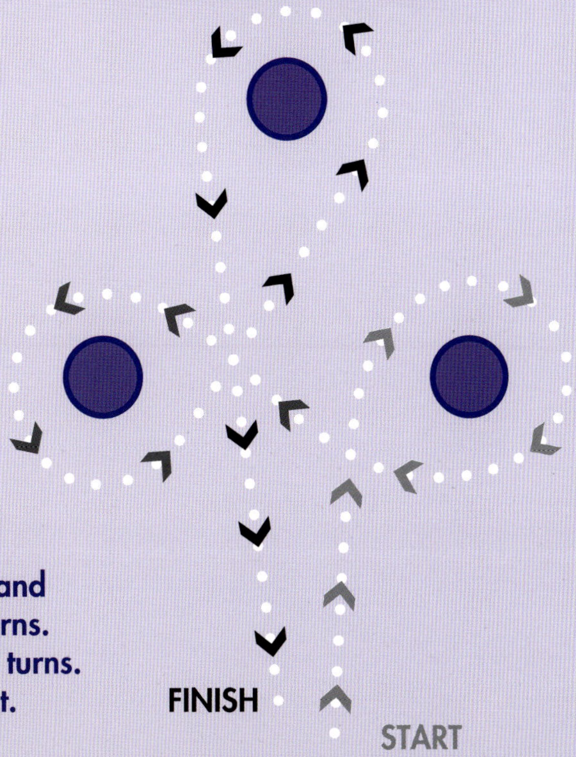

A right-barrel start is one righthand turn followed by two lefthand turns. Most horses are best at lefthand turns. So, racers often start on the right.

Barrel racers must keep good balance so they don't fall off.

Is it dangerous?

DID YOU KNOW?
Some riders use **spurs** to keep their horses focused and fast. But not all horses need them. Most barrel horses love to race!

Riders wear dull spurs so they do not hurt the horse.

Yes. Horses circle the barrels at very fast speeds. The horse or rider could fall at any turn. Riders must keep perfect balance. They must stay calm and in control. Horses need strength and sure footing for tight turns. Pro racing takes outstanding riding skills and a well-trained horse.

How do riders stay safe?

Some riders wear helmets. But it is not required. Most barrel racers wear cowboy hats. But good cowboy boots are a safety *must*. No rider wants a foot stuck in the stirrup. This can cause a nasty spill. Boots with sturdy heels help riders stay in the saddle.

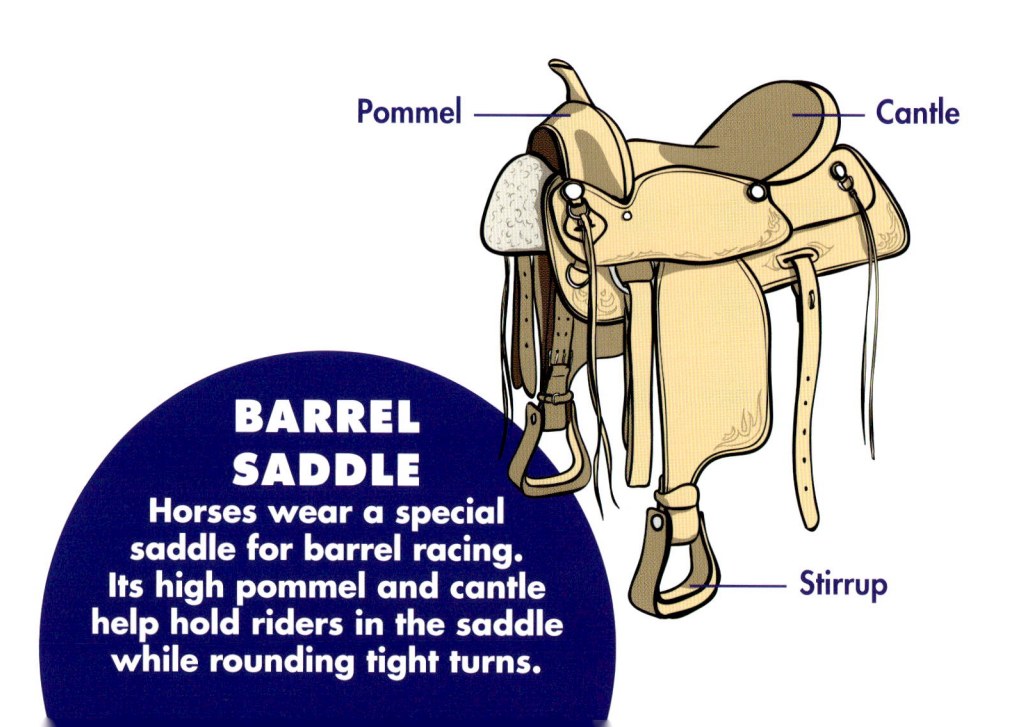

Pommel —— —— Cantle

—— Stirrup

BARREL SADDLE
Horses wear a special saddle for barrel racing. Its high pommel and cantle help hold riders in the saddle while rounding tight turns.

Barrel horses need good racing boots, too. They wear bell boots to protect their hooves.

Bell Boot

How are races timed?

An electronic eye clocks to the hundredth of a second.

Most rodeos use an electronic eye. This casts a beam across the start and finish line. It turns on and off when the horse runs past. The horse enters the arena. The clock starts. Horse and rider circle the barrels. *Hustle home!* They cross the finish line. The clock stops.

DID YOU KNOW?
It's not all about speed. Riders must also complete the cloverleaf pattern to win. Racers who fail to run the correct pattern get a "no score."

What if a rider hits a barrel?

All three barrels must stay standing. Each one knocked down adds five seconds to a rider's time. Race times are very close. A five-second **penalty** is costly. Some riders grab the barrel if it tips. This is gutsy. They could end up in the dirt.

Knocking a barrel over can cause the rider to lose the race.

Is there more than one winner?

Yes. Riders of all skills race together. After the race, riders are grouped into **divisions**. The top division starts with the best time. Each lower division is a half-second slower. There is one winner per division. Times are hundredths of a second apart. That's a close race!

Most barrel races have four divisions of winners. Some have five.

DID YOU KNOW?

In 2017, Hailey Kinsel and her horse, Sister, set a barrel racing record of 13.11 seconds. Who will be the next rider to break it?

ASK MORE QUESTIONS

How much money do barrel racers win?

Is there youth barrel racing near me?

Try a BIG QUESTION: Could I be a barrel racer?

SEARCH FOR ANSWERS

Search the library catalog or the Internet.
A librarian, teacher, or parent can help you.

Using Keywords
Find the looking glass.

Keywords are the most important words in your question.

?

If you want to know about:

- how much barrel racers make, type: BARREL RACING PRIZE MONEY

- youth barrel racing, type: YOUTH BARREL RACING IN [YOUR STATE]

FIND GOOD SOURCES

Here are some good, safe sources you can use in your research.
Your librarian can help you find more.

Books
A Barrel Racer's Dream
by M.D. Ford, 2020.

Barrel Racing
by Rochelle Groskreutz, 2020.

Internet Sites
Britannica Kids: Rodeos
https://kids.britannica.com/students/ article/rodeo/276762
Kids Britannica is an encyclopedia with educational information on many topics. Learn more about rodeos.

Kiddle: Barrel Racing Facts for Kids
https://kids.kiddle.co/Barrel_racing
Kiddle is an online encyclopedia for kids. Search for information on a wide variety of educational topics.

Every effort has been made to ensure that these websites are appropriate for children. However, because of the nature of the Internet, it is impossible to guarantee that these sites will remain active indefinitely or that their contents will not be altered.

SHARE AND TAKE ACTION

Watch barrel racing.
Ask an adult to help you find videos of barrel racing events.

Take horseback riding classes.
Barrel racers are highly skilled riders. Learn the basics first.

Attend a rodeo.
Feel the excitement of barrel racing!

GLOSSARY

alleyway The path a horse runs to enter the arena during a barrel race.

amateur Someone who participates in a sport for fun rather than for money.

breed A certain type of animal or plant.

division One of the groups that barrel racers are separated into; divisions are decided based on a rider's time bracket.

penalty A mark that counts against a score.

professional A person who competes in a sport for money.

spurs The spiked wheels on the heel of a rider's boots.

INDEX

About the Author

Rachel Grack has been writing children's nonfiction for twenty-five years. She lives on a ranch in the heart of rodeo country (southern Arizona). Some evenings, she wanders over to watch her neighbors in friendly roping competitions. A western restaurant in town offers weekly bull riding and mutton busting. But Rachel much prefers a quiet ride on her gentle paint horse, Lady.